STEPHEN ROCHE
MY ROAD TO VICTORY

STEPHEN ROCHE
MY ROAD TO VICTORY

Photographs by Graham Watson
of *Inside Cycling*

Stanley Paul

London Melbourne Auckland Johannesburg

Stanley Paul and Co. Ltd
An imprint of Century Hutchinson Ltd
Brookmount House, 62-65 Chandos Place
Covent Garden, London WC2N 4NW

Century Hutchinson Australia (Pty) Ltd
PO Box 496, 16-22 Church Street, Hawthorn, Melbourne,Victoria 3122

Century Hutchinson New Zealand Limited
191 Archers Road, PO Box 40-086, Glenfield, Auckland 10

Century Hutchinson South Africa (Pty) Ltd
PO Box 337, Bergvlei 2012, South Africa

First published 1987

Copyright © Stephen Roche 1987

Set in Linotron Plantin Light/Helvetica Light Condensed

Design and typesetting by Roger Walker Design Studio

Printed in Great Britain by Scotprint Ltd, Musselburgh, Scotland
Bound by Hunter & Foulis, Edinburgh, Scotland

British Library Cataloguing in Publication Data
Roche, Stephen
My road to victory
1.Roche, Stephen
2.Cyclists—Ireland—Biography
796.6'092'4   GV1051.R6
ISBN 0 09 173738 9

TITLE PAGE
There was a special thrill in this moment of victory. Not only had I
become a world champion but I had achieved something that did not
look likely 600 metres from the finishing line

CONTENTS

WINNING IS NOT EASY

There is something glamorous in the picture of a cyclist on a podium, a yellow jersey on his back, waving to the crowd. It certainly gives the cyclist a good feeling. When I returned to Dublin on the day after I won the Tour de France, the reaction of the people was unbelieveable. An experience that can never be forgotten.

Travelling through Dublin's O'Connell Street, standing on top of a roofless double-decker bus. Being aware that you were the person who had brought a little extra happiness into the lives of so many. That made me feel good. I waved and waved and almost felt like giving a papal salute. It was that kind of feeling.

But now, when I look back on the success and see myself standing in the pink jersey of the Giro, the yellow of the Tour or the rainbow jersey of world champion, I see things differently. What I now see is the life that took me to those victories. The training, the sacrifices and especially the time spent away from my wife Lydia and children Nicolas and Christelle.

Before I left home in early May to ride the Tour of Romandie in Switzerland, Christelle was just a baby, barely at the creeping stage. After Romandie I rode the Giro and the Tour without seeing Nicolas and Christelle, who were in Ireland with Lydia. The next

time I saw Christelle was in Dijon on 25 July, the day I won the yellow jersey from Delgado. What struck me that evening was that my little daughter was walking.

While I am away important things happen at home. You can never make up for what you miss: Christelle only takes her first step once. But this is the life I have chosen for myself and if it is a good life it is so because of the sacrifices.

When I look back over the years and wonder about the things that got me this far, I think the best thing I ever did was to qualify at something else before trying cycling. I was a fairly good Irish amateur in the late 1970s but had no belief in my ability to become a professional, let alone a successful professional.

Sean Kelly was the only Irish professional at the time but we saw him as a superman, something we could never be. Kelly's reputation was awesome and discouraged us from thinking about becoming a professional. So I set about finding a career and began an apprenticeship to be a maintenance fitter.

This suited me for I had always been fascinated with machines and how they work. I served the three years' apprenticeship and then began working as a qualified fitter. All the time I was improving on the bike and was selected to represent Ireland in the Moscow Olympics in 1980.

I thought it would be a good idea to get some experience of riding against the best guys before going to the Olympics and so I decided to spend the six months before the games riding in France. Maybe there was a feeling in the back of my mind that I could get a pro contract in France but it was secondary and I don't think I believed it.

I rode with the famous amateur team ACBB in Paris and had some

good placings at first. I asked if there was any chance of a pro contract, and they said that placings were nothing. So I began to win a few races, my victory in the amateur Paris–Roubaix being the best of all. Peugeot came along with an offer to turn pro and I accepted. I began riding in the pro peloton in February 1981.

Over the last seven years I have had my ups and downs. Times when people thought I would be a champion, times when they were convinced I was not going to make it. Myself, I always believed in my ability. Sure there were problems, illnesses and injuries, things that prevented me from producing my best performances. But as soon as I was well I was always able to do something that showed I had some class.

In 1987 everything fell into place. My health was excellent, there were no worries of any nature. I was ready for a big season and it happened. The fact that it worked out so well was a tribute to the life I have led as a pro. For even when things were 'not' going so well, I accepted the discipline.

My life can be explained in this way. I break my season into parts. The first part is the pre-season training and all races up to Criterium International. On the Sunday night that Criterium International ends I go back to Paris and, with Lydia, I have a fling. This means we stop at a restaurant, have a pizza and an ice cream, things that I would not touch normally. Then we go home.

That is it. The big fling to compensate for three months of intensive racing and training. As I think back on the Tour de France I know that it was those long days, weeks, months of cycling that took me to the Champs Elysées and the podium.

7

THE SPRING CAMPAIGN

Paris–Nice is the first important stage race of the season. They call it the 'race to the sun' but for the riders it is a race where we expect to see snow and feel cold. Even though I don't like the snow and cold, I do better in these conditions than most other riders. Maybe it has something to do with being Irish!

A GOOD START IS...

From the beginning I knew that 1987 was going to be a make or break year for me. I had told myself that if things did not go well I might leave the sport. I do not know if I would have opted out of the peloton but another year like the one I had in 1986 would have made me think very seriously.

1986 had been the worst year of my career. At the end of 1985 I had crashed on the Paris Six-Day track meeting and damaged my knee. I rested the knee, went to see different doctors, got conflicting diagnoses but all through 1986 it affected my performance.

Towards the end of the season I stopped racing and went to a hospital in Paris for X-rays and the specialist there told me that my career was over. Maybe one more season, he said, but not at my best and then it would be finished. My trouble was supposed to be arthritis in the knee joint.

Another specialist at the same hospital looked at the X-rays and confirmed this belief. He too said my career was finished. I believed them. I went home, did not say anything to Lydia, but just counted the money that I had made in cycling. I wanted to see what I would be getting out with.

My own doctor was on holiday and when he returned I immediately went to see him. I brought the X-rays and told him what the specialists had said. He told me they were wrong. The arthritis was normal for a full-time racing cyclist and would not do any harm. Eventually it was decided that I needed only a minor operation to correct the problem in my knee.

That took place in October 1986 and as soon as I left hospital I began to prepare for the following season. I was advised by my doctor to take things very slowly and I listened to the instructions. After the disappointment of 1986 I wanted to prepare correctly for 1987. Sometimes you think you are doing everything correctly but you are not. This time I was and I knew it.

Before the start of the season I trained better than I had ever done in my life. The Italian team for which I rode, Carrera, had supported me well through 1986, when I was not riding well, and I wanted to repay them. I set myself a target of being fully competitive at the time of Liège–Bastogne–Liège in April. That is one of my favourite races and I wanted to do well in it.

But because of the work done during the winter I was competitive much sooner than that. In fact I was going well in the opening races of the season and won the Tour of Valencia in February. What pleased me about that success was that I won a time trial, beating riders like Jean Luc Vandenbroucke and Kelly.

This was the most important season of my career and I had started well.

In the 1987 Paris–Nice I rode well and had the race leader's jersey in St Tropez. You may notice the shaven face. Occasionally I like to show the other riders that I am not the gentle and timid person they think I am – so I let a little beard grow and try to look savage

BAD LUCK AND BAD TACTICS

The two major battles of the spring campaign for me were Paris–Nice and Liège–Bastogne–Liège: the first a good stage race, the second a very good one-day classic. I should have won both but I ended up with neither. I lost Paris–Nice through bad luck and bad tactics; in Liège–Bastogne–Liège there was only bad tactics.

Paris–Nice had been a great race for me up until the final day. I got the race leader's jersey early, lost it to Jean François Bernard and then regained it with one of my bravest rides of the season when attacking from the gun on the St Tropez stage. On the morning of the last day I felt good about my chances of holding on to the leader's jersey.

The morning stage to Nice rarely changed anything and I felt I could beat Kelly (who was second) in the afternoon Col d'Eze time trial. But the morning stage did change things. Near the summit of the Col de Vence I punctured. Although Kelly's team were making a fast tempo I was not too worried, I was sure I could get back on.

With assistance from four team mates I rode strongly after the leaders but at the top I still had not got back. Then, over-reacting, I surged down the descent, leaving three of my team mates behind. We should have stayed together.

I never caught up with the leaders and lost my race lead to Kelly, never to get it back. It was the only leader's jersey I wore in 1987 that I did not have at the end of the race. I hope I never repeat the mistakes I made after the puncture on the Col de Vence.

▲ I panicked in pursuing Kelly and went so fast on the descent from the Col de Vence that I left valuable team mates Schepers, Maechler and Zimmerman behind. Only Leali was with me and although we rode hard, we could not get back. Normally Leali is a really powerful rider but he was not having a good day. It was a bad experience but these things happen in cycling

◄ Punctures can cost important victories. I am third in line in the climb of the Col de Vence on the final day of the Paris–Nice. Leading is Sean Kelly's Kas team mate, Jean Luc Vandenbroucke, then Kelly, then me. A few hundred yards later I would puncture, losing contact with Kelly and, ultimately, losing my race leader's jersey

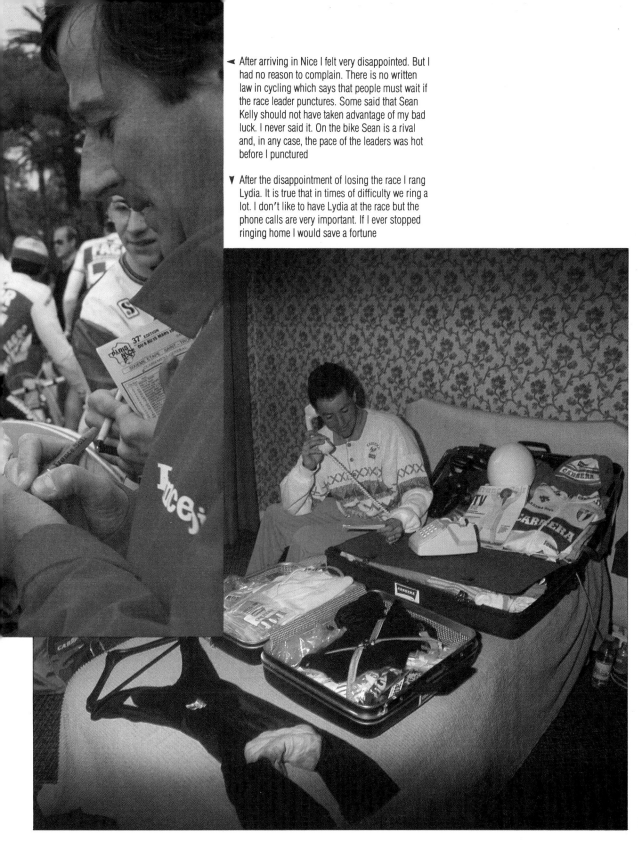

◄ After arriving in Nice I felt very disappointed. But I had no reason to complain. There is no written law in cycling which says that people must wait if the race leader punctures. Some said that Sean Kelly should not have taken advantage of my bad luck. I never said it. On the bike Sean is a rival and, in any case, the pace of the leaders was hot before I punctured

▼ After the disappointment of losing the race I rang Lydia. It is true that in times of difficulty we ring a lot. I don't like to have Lydia at the race but the phone calls are very important. If I ever stopped ringing home I would save a fortune

15

◄ When I look at a peloton this size, I think only of the Milan–San Remo classic. An army of riders like this is fine on a big motorway but Milan–San Remo has a number of climbs where the road is not more than four or five metres wide. You need big elbows to get to the front. I have never won Milan–San Remo but then I am not a champion pusher

▲ My team mate Erich Maechler won the 1987 Milan–San Remo and I was delighted for him. He was supposed to stay with me all through the race but when I saw a break go, I told him to follow. It was the winning break. Erich is the kind of rider who can cope with success. He won Milan–San Remo but it did not change him – he still accepted that he would best serve the team by playing the *domestique's* role. I was happy to shake his hand

17

CAT AND MOUSE
AND CRIQUIELION
Liège–Bastogne–Liège

On the evening that I lost Liège–Bastogne–Liège I drove back to Paris from Liège. Normally I like to drive fast. This evening I could not drive fast. My foot kept jerking on the accelerator, 60 miles per hour and no faster. I was replaying the race in my head, feeling no sympathy for myself as it had been my fault.

My problem began on the night before the race when our Carrera *directeur sportif* Davide Boifava discussed the tactics that I should employ. He knew how badly I wanted to win this race but suggested that I would have 'to be prepared to lose in order to win'.

In other words Boifava wanted me to be less active in a breakaway. Normally when I am in a break I will ride strongly, that is my style. Boifava was telling me that I

Liège–Bastogne–Liège – my favourite classic. At this moment in the 1987 race Claude Criquielion had just attacked, Moreno Argentin was trying to react and I was preparing myself for a counter-attack

tended to do too much and was making it easy for others to beat at the finish.

I could see what he meant and decided that in the race I would be more cagy and try to keep some energy in reserve for the final part of the race. The problem was that in taking Boifava's advice I threw out all that I had learned and believed in for the previous six years.

Generally I have no arguments with anybody in the peloton and if any arise I like to get them sorted out straight away. The way I rode in the final two kilometres was wrong and Criquielion was entitled to be annoyed. But there is no point in carrying on these quarrels, you must forgive and forget.

Criquielion never did forget. When they asked him what he thought of my win in the Tour of Italy, he said I did not beat much. I never found out what he thought of my Tour de France and World Championship victories. He rode both the Tour and Worlds.

19

▲ I joined Criquielion and we worked together until we reached the town of Liège. Then, just one kilometre from the finish, we began playing cagy. I did not want to lead out the sprint, neither did he. It was mostly my fault and I accept full responsibility for the failure it led to.

➤ As Criquielion and I played around, Argentin came from nowhere to beat us on the line. The first I saw of him was 150 metres from the line. I got quite a fright for I was sure I only had Criquielion to beat. This was the most disappointing defeat of my career and Criquielion has not forgiven me for the way I rode

LIVING WITH THE FEAR

► Sean Yates, a good friend and strong rider, tries to wipe away the pain after a crash in this year's Tour de France

▼ Theo de Rooy suffers a fall in Paris–Roubaix. It is a dangerous race and one that I have avoided for the last few years but I would love to ride it and win it

Every time a rider crashes, one thought flashes through my mind – it could have been me. The sport is dangerous and I am conscious of the fact that I have a wife and two children and responsibilities. You always try not to take risks. But you will crash anyway and you only hope that it will not be serious.

I pay a lot of money for insurance but I worry how the insurance company will adjudicate on my injury if it is serious. If, tomorrow, I suffer an injury that prevents me from racing again,

▲ Thierry Marie is another casualty of the race they call *L'enfer du Nord*

◄ Rider 238 explains his problems to the journalists. From this angle, the explanation is easy

how much will I get? My experience leads me to believe that cyclists do not get as much as they should.

In the early season classics, particularly those over cobbles (Tour of Flanders and Paris–Roubaix) crashing is common. The weather is often bad and when the cobbles get slippery they are very dangerous. I try to avoid these races. But I plan to ride Paris–Roubaix in 1988.

You do find the same fellows falling off, just as you find the same fellows puncturing. There is a reason for this: riders who are struggling to keep up will be more tired than the others, more liable to crash. Riders who are struggling will ride on gravel rather than face the wind. The stronger ones can avoid these things.

23

Laurent Fignon looks for his bike after a crash in this year's Tour de France

I WANTED TO WIN

Officially, the position in the Carrera team before the Giro d'Italia was that Roberto Visentini and I were joint leaders. I was supposed to support him if he had the leader's jersey and he was supposed to support me if I had it. I believed that this would be the case even if, deep down, I had some suspicions.

There was also the fact that I was in very good form. My final preparation race for the Giro was the Tour of Romandie, which I won. Overall I had raced well for Carrera during the first four months of the season: winning the Tours of Valencia and Romandie, coming second in Criterium International and Liège–Bastogne–Liège, and well up in many other races.

All through these months Roberto had given me no help and had done nothing himself. Before the Giro he was saying that in his opinion I was more interested in winning the Tour de France than the Giro. That was never how I saw it. I would never go to a race as hard and as long as the Giro and not be trying my hardest to win.

My suspicions that the team might be more behind Roberto than me were aroused from the very earliest days of the race. When he did a good ride the reaction in the team made me feel that he was the man they wanted to win. This puzzled me for Roberto does not always treat his team mates well and he had done nothing for them earlier in the season.

When I led the race during the first week he did not help me in any way but continually stayed on my back wheel. Wherever I went he followed; he did nothing to help me and was not going to do anything to help me. I knew where I stood.

For the first ten days I had the leader's jersey. Then on the tenth stage I performed badly, partly as a result of a crash three days previously and partly through nervousness, in the San Marino time trial.

Visentini performed very well, he jumped above me and led the race by two minutes and 42 seconds. Immediately the Italians presumed that the race was over. I would now work for Visentini and it was said that he would work for me in the Tour de France.

This was the official statement from the team but I knew that Visentini had already booked holidays for July when the Tour would be on, and had no intention of working for me. On the night after the time trial, my loyal team mate Eddy Schepers spoke to me about the race, telling me that I could not accept defeat, that I had come to win and that I must continue to try.

This is what I felt too but I had not the courage to say it out like that. I agreed with Eddy and the two of us discussed where I might attack to get the jersey back from Visentini. The race was not over and, more than anything else, that was the conclusion to our discussions.

When Visentini won the leader's jersey from me in San Marino he had reason to celebrate for everyone in Italy believed he had won the Giro. It was deemed that a second page in the history of the 1987 Giro had begun and that the first page, concerning Roche in the pink jersey, was now history. Everybody saw it this way except me

THE SAPPADA AFFAIR

When Eddy and I discussed how I might get the pink jersey back from Visentini we decided that we had to go for it on a stage when he would not be expecting me to try. Stage 16 to Marmolada was very hard and looked an obvious place to attack but the previous day's stage also presented opportunities and Visentini would not be expecting anything to happen on the road to Sappada.

On the descent after the first climb on this stage there were numerous attacks and I went away with two riders, Ennio Salvador and Jean Claude Bagot. Carrera's *directeur sportif* Davide Boifava was furious and drove up to tell that I must stop. He ordered the entire Carrera team to lead the pursuit.

This made me angry because I felt it was in Carrera's interests to force all the other teams in the race to pursue me. The war was on. I told Boifava that if the other teams did not chase me I would win the stage by ten minutes and Carrera would still win the Giro.

But it was clear that Carrera preferred their Italian to win the ▷

▲ The pursuit of Roche is still on! On this section of the climb my Carrera team mate Claudio Cappucci tried to tow Visentini and the peloton up to me. Earlier in the race Claudio had asked me for a signed pink jersey for his girlfriend. I gave it to him. When the conflict between Visentini and me happened, he sided with Visentini. But on the day the race ended he still had the nerve to ask me for another pink jersey. This time he did not get it

◄ A moment from the fateful day to Sappada, the day I took the leader's jersey back from Visentini. Here Roberto takes a drink from his bidon. You know something serious is happening because of the big men at the front: Breukink, Winnen, Giupponi, Argentin and Corti. You know Visentini is in trouble because he has no team mates around him. The concern among the leaders stems from the fact that I am still on my long breakaway ride

▲ Visentini suffered because of the efforts to pull me back. Eddy Schepers stayed close to him but never helped him, just rode behind him. It was nice to know that there was one Carrera rider supportive of what I was doing

► Another serious moment on the stage to Sappada. I had been away for most of the day and just as I was being recaptured there was a counter-attack by Phil Anderson and Jean François Bernard, on either side of me and I had to go with them

▷ race and I was not going to accept that. Second place was as good as twentieth – in other words, no good. Boifava even sent Patrick up to tell me that I must stop. I asked Patrick what he thought and he said I should continue. I agreed and did just that.

The Carrera team exhausted itself in the pursuit of its own rider and Visentini then enlisted the help of another Italian team, Attila, to chase me down. Eventually I was recaptured but when the counter-attacks came I had the strength to hang on. For this I must thank Eddy as I was really tired. Without his presence and encouragement I would not have kept my place.

On the last climb to Sappada Boifava told Eddy to go back to Visentini but Eddy said he was going to stay with me. Visentini ended up losing over six minutes on the climb. I got the jersey but only by a few seconds. Had I not got the jersey I feel Eddy and I might have been sent home.

It was a hard, hard day for me but the objective of the day had been achieved and that was the only thing that counted.

◄ The race to Sappada is truly on. Robert Millar leads the charge, his green jersey denoting that he was the strongest climber. When I was in trouble with the Italians, Bob was a great help. I never asked him, he just saw what was happening and decided to help in whatever way he could

▼ I was one of the few people smiling after I took the jersey back from Roberto in Sappada. I sensed that many people were annoyed at what had happened but I kept smiling, blowing kisses at everyone and decided that if there were some out there who supported me, I was going to keep them on my side

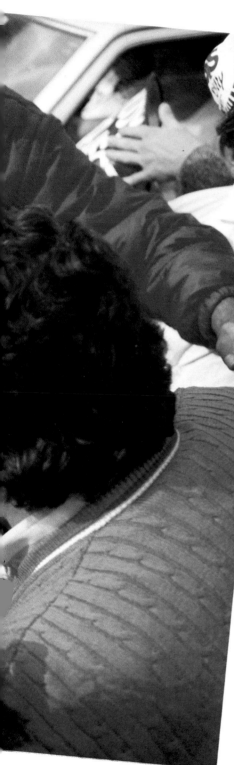

Visentini was a little upset at what happened on the road to Sappada. The journalists asked what had gone wrong and he replied that he did not know but 'certain people' would be going home that evening. He meant me, Eddy and my mechanic Patrick Valcke. I felt that because I had the jersey Carrera would not send me home. I was in two minds about the prospect – it would cost me the Giro if I was sent home but I knew it would be dangerous to stay

▲ Patrick escorts me away from the podium after getting the jersey in Sappada. Over the next week I would need a police escort through these crowds. The finish areas were chaotic in Italy, worse than the Tour de France, with no restrictions on who was allowed to get close to the riders

► The morning after Sappada. I was in no doubt how the Italians felt about my exploits. I only had to read the newspapers. The front page headline of *La Gazzeta dello Sport* says 'Roche Attacks Visentini'

▼ On the morning after Sappada there were some who actually wanted my autograph. In Italy I never stopped trying to convince the Italians that I was not a bad boy. I think every single person who asked for an autograph during that race got it

TEAM ROCHE!

There were three of us: Patrick Valke, Eddy Schepers and myself. No matter what, we were together. Patrick has been my mechanic since my first year as a pro and we get on really well together. He understands me and is invaluable, for as well as being a good mechanic he can give me massage when necessary.

Because he was so much on my side in the Giro he was relegated to Carrera's second team car. Patrick is my second opinion on all the questions about equipment; what wheels should be used in a certain time trial, what gears on a certain mountain and so on. He will offer his advice but never insist that I accept it.

He knows that if I disagree I will act on my judgement. He understands that he can only put doubts in my mind by insisting, so he never will. During the Giro he was on the same wavelength as Eddy and I.

It is odd that Eddy and I became good friends during 1986 when I was not going well. Maybe Eddy saw something in me for he was prepared to ride for me. At the end of last season Carrera were pre-

pared to let Eddy go but I pleaded with them to keep Eddy, whom I considered a super team rider.

This season Eddy was exceptional. The important thing in the Giro was that he encouraged me to fight back when Visentini took the jersey. I thought that I should fight back but without Eddy saying that I must, I don't know if I would have done. Then, when I made my attack at Sappada, Eddy was strong at the end of the stage and played a big part in making sure that I stayed with the leaders.

One Italian newspaper had nicknames for the three of us. Eddy was 'the rebel' for rebelling against Boifava and taking my side. I was called 'Judas' for 'betraying' Visentini, and Patrick, poor Patrick was called 'Satan'. All the trouble made us stick closer together.

◄ After Sappada there was a long mountainous stage to Marmolada where the crowds on the climbs would be enormous. I could hear people shouting things that were not nice and I prayed that their arms would not be long enough to reach me

▲ Visentini tried a few attacks but he was not getting away from me. Every time he moved, I moved my pink jersey up to him. Each time the TV helicopter could see me closing the gap on Visentini, my popularity in Italy sunk lower. Maybe I was over-reacting to Visentini's attacks but I was determined he was not going to get the pink jersey back and that was it

Bob surveys the next part of the climb as he and ►
Eddy continue to lead me. That day Visentini rode
close to me, which was fine. It meant that if I was
punched and brought down, the chances were
that I would be able to take him with me

◄ Without Bob Millar and Eddy Schepers I would
not have got through the Giro. On the Marmolada
stage they rode at either side of me to protect me
from the possibility of a punch from a fan. Riding
shotgun, if you like. Bob suffered on this day
because Eddy was going so well

Eddy and Bob are still doing their job, I am just ►
behind them and then Visentini. Note the gestures
of the supporters on the roadsides. Italians talk a
lot with their hands. Many of them were fair but
there were always some who would call me
'Judas' and scream at Visentini to 'get me'

All the time during the Giro Davide Boifava, my *directeur* and Visentini spoke to the Italian journalists and gave their side of the story. After the Sappada I was forbidden to speak with the journalists but I knew that silence from me was a confession of guilt. I was not prepared to stay silent and I did not

Roberto Visentini had the Italian people behind him, his team and his sponsor. He had everything going for him. From the beginning I said I would not do anything against him but he never helped me in the races we had ridden before the Giro. I will work for anybody who is prepared to work for me

Giro organizer Vincenzo Torriani whispering encouragement? Actually Torriani was good, he directed the race very fairly and he kept saying 'Bravo, Stephano' every time we met. Sometimes organizers like to see foreigners winning because it gives prestige to their race

▼ Bob and Marino Lejarreta break clear. Both were really strong and Lejarreta rode all three major tours in 1987. He would do much better if he were prepared to take the initiative more. He preserves his strength until it is too late to use it

THE TIFOSI

Throughout my life I have maintained that you must forgive and forget. I do not forget that many Italians who came to the roadside in this year's Giro cheered for me. Those who did not were instantly forgiven.

I think the Giro is a great tour and one that suits my talents. I would like to go back and win it again and it is my intention to ride the Giro in 1988. I like to think that by the end of the 1987 race I had convinced the vast majority of people in Italy that I was a worthy winner of their race.

Maybe it is a weakness of Italian cycling that people in Italy think that an Italian must win the Giro. Because of this the course for the race is often designed to suit the best Italian racers. In recent years this has meant that the Giro route has not always been as severe as it could be.

The long-term result of this is that the best Italians are not being pushed far enough. Of course I thought that this Giro was severe enough.

46

A moment to remember from the Giro! The town of Pila, Bob has won the stage, I have finished second and strengthened my grip on the leader's jersey and here we are receiving the applause of the crowd. Or are we? In fact the crowd were shouting and booing and I am politely asking them to stay quiet. It upset me that they were all not happy about my success but I still had a job to get on with

▲ After the tension in our team throughout the race there was a return to normality in the last few days. Some of the lads actually rode harder than they had ever done for me, if only to prove they were supportive. Here the Carrera jerseys are controlling things as the peloton enters the finishing circuit

◄ I did not wear the sunglasses in an attempt to hide from the Italians but to get protection from the sun. I believe strongly that riders should not be photographed wearing sunglasses because it detracts from the sport. I wear them in the early part of the stage, never at the finish, and I take them off if there is a photographer around

► Other things happened at the Giro. Riders still had to attend to the call of nature. What you see here, riders peeing at the side of the road, is something I try to avoid because when you stop you have to ride a little bit hard to catch up. I prefer to pee as I move, keeping my place close to the front

When Visentini and I were not acting out our battle, Paulo Rosola was proving himself the exceptional sprinter of the Giro. He is really fast and a bit of a character – he has a little ponytail and is always ready to joke. In one bunch sprint on this year's Giro he warned me to move away from the front: 'This is for sprinters, Stephen,' he said. The next day there was a climb and as I went past him I told him to get lost: 'This is for the climbers, Paulo.' In bike racing you need characters like Rosola

You presume the weather on the summer tours is ➤
going to be hot but there are always days when it
rains heavily or gets cold. I would never say that I
like the rain or cold, just as the Colombians
would never say they love the intense heat. But I
know that in the rain and cold I will ride well, just
as they will ride well in the heat

◄ Moreno Argentin rode well in the Giro, winning
two stages, but is not a good stage-race rider. He
is at his best in the one-day races of his choice,
for example Liège–Bastogne–Liège and the World
Championship. His performances in these two
races have been outstanding

◄ I have always got on well with Robert Millar. He is
quiet but once you know him he is very sound. He
is also straight . I have wanted to get back on the
same team as he since we used to ride together at
Peugeot. Next season we will be together again at
Fagor

In the tours of Italy and France you will see riders undressing as they ride. It can be cold in the morning, at the start of the stage, and then as the day gets hot people want to take off their undervest. I like to leave an undervest on at all times as it offers protection if I crash. Notice the suntans of Millar, Yates and Regis Clere – cycling tans!

▼ It was hectic all the way to the finish. Although I had the race almost won at this point, I felt a crack in my forks and asked Eddy to ride directly behind on the descent. I made it to the finish without the cracked forks causing me any problem

By the time we left the mountains in the Giro the major questions had been asked and answered. Many of those Italians who had been unhappy when I took the jersey from Visentini had come round and were admitting that I was the best rider in the race. The Carrera team came round too and were very good for the last four or five days

LE TOUR DE TRIOMPHE

The peloton speeds off into the mist and another Tour de France. I like to ride at the front of the pack so I can see what is happening and try to tune in to the plots that are being hatched and executed.

I started out curious, wondering how things would go after Italy. I spoke with Jacques Anquetil who had, in his time, won the Giro/Tour double in the same season. He said that the Giro would enable me to suffer better than most riders in the Tour. Anquetil also said that when he won the Giro, he never went as well in that year's Tour

HOPING—NOT EXPECTING

From the time that I won Paris–Nice in my first professional season, 1981, people said that I could one day win the Tour de France. But then there were problems with injuries and some of the biggest disappointments I experienced were in the Tour. I thought I could do well in 1984 but crashed two days before the first mountain stage and injured my leg. I just could not climb as a result.

In 1985 I was in good physical condition and rode well to finish third overall behind Bernard Hinault and Greg LeMond. The stage win at the summit of Col d'Aubisque proved that on certain days I could climb really well and, generally, I was consistent in that tour.

That third place should have set things up for a really good Tour in 1986 but my year was ruined by an injury to my knee which I had picked up three months before the season began. I was foolish in 1986, trying to compete when I was not fit. I rode the Giro but was unable to climb because of my injury.

Still I went on and rode the Tour de France. It was a devastating experience. In the Pyrenees I lost 28 minutes on one stage. Spectators pushed me and I was glad of the assistance. I do not know why I continued in the race except that I hate having to abandon any race, especially the Tour.

So though I had enjoyed a really good start to the 1987 season and was totally free of injury, I did not consider myself likely to win the Tour. Even 'after the success in Italy, I only hoped that I could ride a good Tour. I never said I would win the race, but a number of journalists said it and I was regarded as one of the favourites.

For me one of the big questions was how I would recover from the race in Italy. It has been a mental battle as much as a physical one and I just did not know how much I had taken out of myself. On the Saturday night that the Giro ended I drove back to Paris immediately after the race finished.

I did not feel that Carrera wished me to stick around for celebrations and I was glad to drive home that evening. As it turned out it was a very enjoyable journey. I drove the car of Bruno and Corrine, friends of Lydia's and mine.

Bruno and Corrine had driven to Italy just before the race ended. The day before the race ended they stayed up most of the night painting the road. They had a map of Italy, showing Roche in pink, and a map of France, showing Roche in yellow. The Italians did not think much of their taste. When the race ended they were very tired and I decided I would drive their Peugeot 104 back to Paris and let them sleep in the back.

Eddy drove my car back to Paris and when we arrived home, at about 4.30 in the morning, we had our own little celebration. It was a good night. I was pleased to come

◄ Berlin was an unusual starting point for a Tour de France but the city put on a magnificent show for the race. Their presentation of the riders was real Lido stuff, very classy, and the crowds that came to the roadside were enormous

▷

▷ out of Italy with the one thing I wanted – victory.

But I was tired. There was a civic reception for me in Dublin and I had to go home. I used the trip to Dublin as an excuse to spend a few days relaxing because the Tour was just two weeks away. After the reception it was reported that I had returned to France but, in fact, I had stayed in Dublin for a few quiet days of rest.

That meant hours spent working on an old car, which is my favourite hobby. After what had happened in Italy I found the time spent fixing up the car was very relaxing. It was just what I needed. I had no plans to ride any races between the two tours.

I had no idea how my form would hold up for the Tour de France and could only hope. My plan was to use the first ten days of the tour to ride myself in and then hope that I would feel the benefits of having ridden the Giro. I had worked out that my first major effort would come in the Futuroscope time trial on the tenth day.

I went into the Tour de France hoping, not expecting.

➤ The team trial is one of the most difficult tests in cycling. In an individual test you are on your own and you go as fast as you can. It is the same on a climb. But in the team time trial you go as fast as you can but also you go as fast as your strongest team mate can. A lot of riders destroy their performances because they fear losing contact. In the Berlin team time trial I felt strong and Carrera achieved a good victory. It is an event that suits my abilities

➤ Five of the Carrera bunch. From the left Pedersen, Zimmerman, Maechler, Bontempi and Ghirotto. The team rode strongly to defend Maechler when he had the yellow jersey in the first week but when it came to the mountains Eddy was the only one to do anything for me

IS THERE A PLACE FOR WIFE OR GIRLFRIEND?

For me, there is no place on the Tour for Lydia. Being in the race does not mean that I ride that day's stage and relax – it is a 24-hour day and I would not be happy trying to look after Lydia if she were around.

Twice this year Lydia turned up at races. Once in Italy when I was down and needed to see her. But I did not ask and she did not say she was coming. She just turned up and then tried not to interfere with my routine or the team's. Lydia fully understands cycling's ways as

◄ The people who wait at the side of the road for the Tour to pass are a part of the scenery and when they are not there we miss them. As we pass we may not notice any particular little group of people but we are conscious of the size of the crowds

▼ Urs Zimmerman with his girlfriend Caroline at the end of a stage. Caroline was working on this year's race and able to see Urs quite often

her brother Thierry used to be a good amateur and her family are interested in the sport.

Imagine the scene when a wife or girlfriend turns up. We finish the stage at 4.30, return to the hotel at around 5.30; shower and massage takes us up to 6.30–7.0. Then there is the evening meal and that can go on until 9.0–9.30. The evening meal is important because it enables the team to get together as a group.

After the evening meal it is time for bed. So where is the wife or girlfriend fitted in? At the end of the day we would have the neglected lady asking 'Don't you love me any more?'

There is also the fact that if one member of the team has a wife or girlfriend around it can damage the ambience within the group. Others see him and his lady friend together and feel a little jealous; it makes them miss their own ladies all the more.

▲ The *domestiques* go back to the team cars for
water. I am valuable because I can win but I can
not win without the help of my *domestiques*. I
can ask Eddy to go back to the team car for water,
glucose, a time check, a change of bike, without
him I would be lost

▲ Claude Criquielion receives medical help during
the Tour. Probably an anti-inflammatory injection,
when you crash or develop some kind of injury in
the Tour, the immediate reaction is to try to get to
the stage finish. Then you can see if the injury is
severe enough to force you out. Spend five
minutes talking to the doctor during the stage and
you may never get to the finish within the time
limit

➤ Because of the huge coverage the Tour gets, every
team wants its share of the publicity and there is
always somebody who is prepared to attack.
Whether the attack succeeds depends upon who
you are. Sometimes it is not a compliment to be
given a little rein by the pack: 'Ah, he doesn't
count, let him go'

A FRIEND'S BAD LUCK

The moment Sean Kelly was forced to abandon this year's Tour everybody knew that there was more to the peloton than dog-eat-dog. When I heard that he had crashed I went to see how he was. He was back on his bike and I thought that all he needed was a little cheering up.

I reminded him how the Tour was such a great holiday – three weeks of free hotels, a tour around France, lovely scenery, great food and plenty of rest. After a while it dawned on me that he was not going to be all right. That was sad because I do not like to see anybody having to pull out of the Tour, not even a fellow that I might not like.

Sean's crash was a blow. He is not just another rider but a fellow that I am particularly fond of. We have been close for a good few years and he is one of the best friends I have made in cycling. On the bike we can be rivals but we strive to be the best in the world, not the best of the Irish.

◄ A big pack cruising along. It looks so easy. Sometimes when the speed is at its lowest there can be bad crashes as people get careless. It is often more painful to fall when you are travelling slowly than when you crash at high speed. The crash that knocked Kelly out of this year's Tour took place when the bunch was taking things easily

► On the Tour Kelly and I always find an opportunity to talk. After his crash there was a genuine sympathy for him in the peloton. The pictures of Sanders and da Silva pushing him up the hill, of Kelly admitting to himself that the Tour was over and of him sitting dejectedly in the ambulance bring back the sadness we felt for him that day

67

► And what of masseuses on the Tour? Shelley Verses and April Wilburn worked for the Toshiba and 7-Eleven teams on this year's race. I have had a massage from Shelley and she is very good at her job. I have no experience of April. Both Shelley and April are from the US and their involvement in the sport is a typical American development. I do not know if it is a good thing

▼ Jacques Goddet, on the right, directed his last Tour this year. The man is something else. He was very close to the riders. When he came to you in the morning and asked if you were OK, you knew he cared. His sympathy was for the riders and that is why we had so much respect for him. We need the Tour and it is men like Jacques Goddet who have made it

Shane Sutton of the English-based ANC team, who rode the Tour for the first time, experiences what every cyclist has at one time or other experienced. Hanging on to the back of the peloton until you can hang on no more. It is a miserable feeling for once you let go, there is no comeback. My memory of this feeling goes back to the Dauphine Libère race of 1982 when this happened to me almost every day

> Of the people who work with cycling teams, the mechanics are very important. Ask any of the top riders, all of whom will have their own mechanics. I would not want anybody going near my bike except Patrick, who is super. He would work twenty-four hours a day and sleep, for him, is an interruption. On the Tour, mechanics work harder than anybody

▲ 'Didi' Thurau's expression tells much about the Tour. Thurau is regarded as a playboy within the peloton but you would not know it from this picture of him. As a rider he has a huge amount of class, could be one of the very best if he could remain consistent in his dedication

➤ Another rider with a fair amount of class, Malcolm Elliott. He could have made a bigger impact on the sport if he had spent his early professional years competing on the Continent. But Elliott is a star in England, just as Thurau is a star in West Germany, and they have not been helped by the acclaim they receive at home

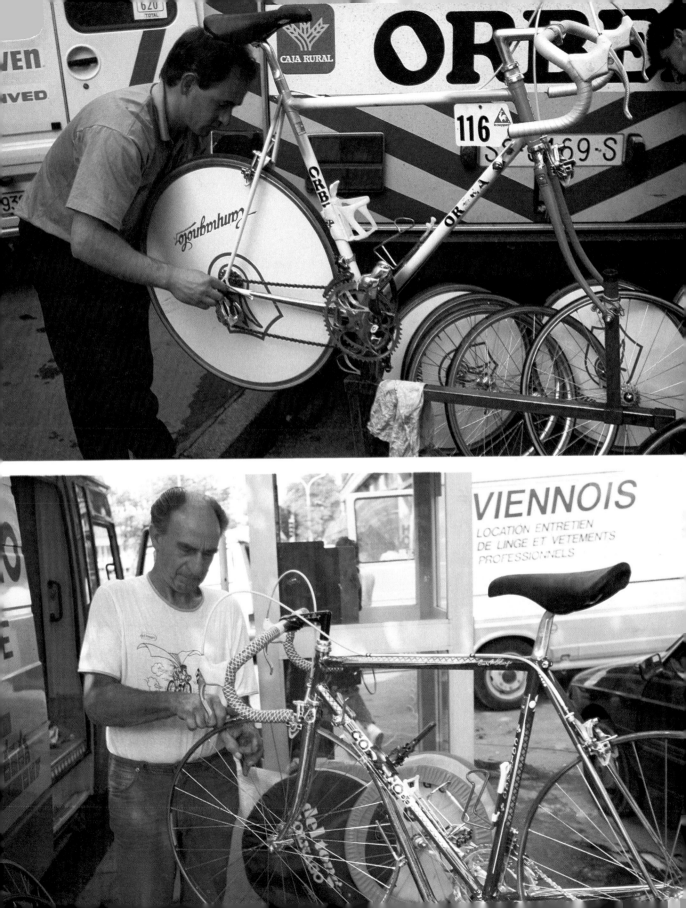

ENTERING THE UNKNOWN

After twelve days of the Tour my hopes of winning were still alive. I knew that my form was good because of my performances in the prologue, when I was third, in the team time trial which Carrera won, and finally in the Futuroscope time trial which I won.

But I still did not feel any confidence. How could I? Each year that the Tour de France had entered the Pyrenees before the Alps I had climbed badly. Maybe there were reasons for that but I was very cautious about my chances on the first mountain stage from Bayonne to Pau.

◄ The journey into the Pyrenees has begun and the climbers are at the front; from left, Lauritzen, Criquielion, Millar, Roux and Herrera. I am near enough for my own comfort but recently I have discovered that sometimes it is easier to ride at the front on the climbs than it is to be in sixth or seventh place

People speak of the differences between the mountain ranges. Some riders like the Alps, others prefer the Pyrenees, I would probably go for the Dolomites in Italy before the two of them. Because I had experiences in the Pyrenees during the Tours of 1983, 1984 and 1986 I could not be sure of surviving this time.

But I thought of what I did in Italy, how well I had climbed on the really difficult mountain stages, and I tried to tell myself that everything would be fine. I was worried about what the specialist climbers would do. Delgado and Millar had done well in the time trials at Futuroscope and they always did well in the Pyrenees.

The Columbians had a habit of riding hard on the first Pyrenean stage and that was a worry too. I did not think that the race leader Charly Mottet would get over the mountains with the best and I did not consider him a potential Tour winner.

But, most of all, I worried about how I would perform. Nothing that I had done previously assured me that everything would go OK. I could only hope, for although my Tour chance seemed as good as anybody else's, I was entering the unknown.

◄ The fact that I climbed to Luz Ardiden in the company of Millar proved that not only was my form good but I was going to be competitive in the mountains as well. It was a relief to have survived because on the stage to Luz Ardiden, the second Pyrenean day, I was all out to maintain my position

People sat on the road and tried to block the Tour, because they wanted to protest against the use of nuclear power. The photographers protested against the conditions under which they had to work on the Tour. There are always protests. Nobody doubts that they are justified but, for me, it is sad that the Tour is used in this way. The Tour is free to the public, that is one of the great things about the race. But it is because it is free that the protesters can disrupt it. Football matches are not used, neither are tennis tournaments, but because the Tour is free it is a target

Two things pleased me especially about this year's Tour. One was winning the long time trial to Futuroscope and so receiving the mounted and studded map of France which went to each stage winner. The other was my climbing: it was better than anything I had achieved before and there were times when I was strong enough to climb from the front

◄ Climbing at the same pace as Lucho Herrera can be one of the most painful ways of spending an afternoon. From the foot of the climb to the summit there is no one to touch him so we must make sure that when Lucho gets to the climb he is either badly placed or tired. If he is alongside, the only way to climb with him is to stay tight on his back wheel. Give him even one yard and you will never get it back

▲ Neither is it a joy to be sitting behind the other great Colombian, Fabian Parra, on a Pyrenean climb. Jean Claude Bagot does not look comfortable! I have always rated Parra very highly as a bike man in that he is far more complete than Lucho and he understands European cycling better than his more famous countryman

Eating constitutes a big part of the cyclist's day, whether in the evening after a stage or out on the road during one. I believe that the team meal is a very important get together and that each rider should turn up properly dressed, i.e. in the official team gear. It is also an opportunity for the riders to prove their commitment to the sponsor and is an opportunity that should be taken. Out on the road the feed zone can be chaotic and dangerous. As Patrick (Valcke) stands and waits it looks so simple, but when you see the ANC team helper searching out his riders in the peloton you get an idea of the confusion

◄ Hampsten is an excellent climber and always looks at his ease. Things did not go well for him this year, which was a surprise to me. I thought he would be one of the real danger men. I imagine he suffered under the pressure of being a team leader in the Tour de France

► Teun Van Vliet was in a bad way at the summit of Luz Ardiden and recuperated quickly to tell journalists the story of his adventure. He tried to win the stage but was caught when in the lead halfway up to Luz Ardiden. I have always liked Teun, he rides honestly when he is in a break with you and, more importantly, he shares my interest in old cars

▼ Victory at Luz Ardiden fell to Dag Otto Lauritzen, a very strong rider but probably too heavy in the legs to be a Tour winner. Dag almost came to my team for next season. He would have fitted in well

Seeing Irish support on a roadside in France or Italy does wonders for the morale. It is amazing what some people will go through to support you. Even on a race as long as the Tour you may see the same tricolour in a different part of France for each of the race's 26 days. I thought the ROCHE '87 – U2 – KELLY '88 was very clever

▼ With Kelly forced out, there were then three Irishmen. From left Paul Kimmage, Martin Earley and myself. I have always liked Paul and Martin, they are good lads. They have settled well in the peloton. They have never begrudged Sean and me what we have achieved

▲ After the Pyrenees the Tour heads for the Alps. The stages between the two mountain ranges are generally over rolling countryside. This year it was different with a stage finish at the summit of a seven-kilometre climb overlooking the town of Millau. The Systeme-U team of race leader Charly Mottet tried to dominate on the climb but they lost. It was a good climb for me, further encouragement after the Pyrenees

► The white slopes of Mont Ventoux and the lone figure of a rider making his way to the top. The mountain time trial to the summit of the Ventoux began the final week of the race and narrowed the list of potential winners to just four; Jean François Bernard, Pedro Delgado, Charly Mottet and I

The rivals–
Jean François
Bernard

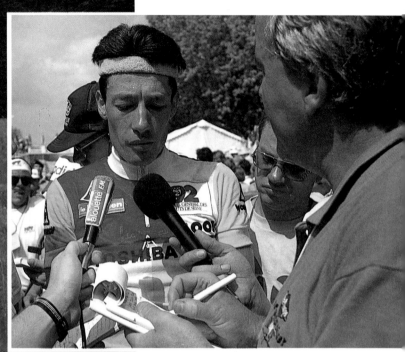

Jean François Bernard is definitely a rider for the future. He will improve and his time trials are exceptional. He is good in the mountains and will get better. It was said that he was unlucky in this year's Tour, getting a puncture when he had the yellow jersey and then having a problem with his chain. But I think it is stupid to see the Tour in this way. I could say that Bernard was five minutes down at the summit of the Aubisque on the second Pyrenean stage and if he was considered a real threat at that time, he would never have got back. Bernard must forget about criticizing others and making excuses for himself. He should pay attention to the fact that at the end of the season there were not many riders who wanted to ride in his team. He must mature

The rivals—Charly Mottet

Charly Mottet was riding very well in the Tour. He is a good rider but possibly a little over-rated. Charly is always looking for his form, it is about to come or it has just gone but he never has it. Of the leading contenders I did not worry too much about Charly. I felt that he would never climb as well as people like Delgado. When there is a nice, steady tempo on a climb Charly is fine but he cannot react when there is an acceleration. The stage to Millau showed that Charly was going to have problems. The Systeme-U team controlled things for Charly until five kilometres from the summit but then, when others put on the pressure, he was left behind. Not a future winner of the Tour

If anybody else was going to win the race, it had to be Pedro Delgado. He was a good rival. During the first 12 days on the flat he hid in the peloton but that is normal for a climber and I do not criticize him. But once the race moved into the mountains he was on his terrain and rode a very good race: always at the front, always ready to attack. When he went there was very little I could do. He can accelerate on the climbs as only the true climber can. When he went on Alpe d'Huez and, a day later, on La Plagne I could only watch him go. As well as being a dangerous rival, Delgado was also a nice lad

ELIMINATING BERNARD

All through the Tour my strategy was simply to keep my hopes alive. Each day I tried not so much to win the Tour as to make sure that I did not lose it, knowing that with each day others would lose their chance. Through the first two and a half weeks I had achieved this objective and as the Tour entered the final week I was third overall and in a very good position.

Then on the first mountain test of the final week, Jean François Bernard produced an exceptional performance in the Ventoux time trial. I had performed okay on the Ventoux, fifth at two minutes 19 seconds behind Bernard. But he was now the race leader and was two minutes 34 seconds ahead of me.

The fact that I was in second place overall did not make any difference. Bernard was now in a very strong position and I sensed that if he could gain the confidence

I knew that Bernard was a threat and was prepared to ride hard at the front of the breakaway group to got along of him. Eddy rode hard as well, so did Fignon and Mottet. But I could not give it everything because I knew that Delgado would attack on the final climb, the Côte de Chalimont. He did and I had just enough reserves to go with him. He was stronger, so I bluffed by riding at his side rather than behind him. This gave him the impression that I was going well

that would come with a couple of days in the yellow jersey, then he would be next to impossible to beat.

It was also clear that he had made enormous efforts on the Ventoux and there was a chance that he would be vulnerable on the next day. Knowing that he might be tired and fearing that he would grow confident if he survived for a few days in yellow, I was pleased to hear that the Systeme-U team were planning to attack Bernard at the first feeding station on the next day's stage.

The stage was from Valreas to Villard des Lens and the first feed came at Leoncel. Charly Mottet, the best placed Systeme-U rider, was from the region and he knew that there would be confusion at Leoncel because of the narrow roads through the town. I was aware of the plan and got myself ready to be a part of it.

As luck would have it, Bernard punctured near the summit of the previous climb, the Tourniol, and had only just rejoined the peloton when the attack came. He was badly placed and found himself in the chasing group when the bunch split.

Fignon, Gayant and Mottet, all Systeme-U, worked hard to distance Bernard, as did Eddy and I. People wondered whether Bernard would have lost time if it was not for the puncture. Maybe he would not have missed the split at Leoncel but I am sure that he would have lost time later in the stage.

But they are the ifs and buts of the Tour and every rider has his own ifs and buts. The only thing that mattered was that at the finish in Villard des Lens I was the new race leader and Jean François Bernard had lost four minutes and 16 seconds. Bernard had been eliminated. Now, he could not win 93 the Tour.

I have always found Alpe d'Huez especially hard. It is not my kind of climb, too irregular. I like a climb where the ascent is even and you do not have to change rhythm too often. So when I won the yellow jersey at Villard des Lens there was worry as well as joy – worry that I would lose it the next day at Alpe d'Huez. I dug in behind Lejarreta and, later Loro and Bernard but lost the jersey by 24 seconds. A disappointment but the Tour was not lost

When Delgado went on the first slopes of La Plagne I did not even consider going with him. His attack was too much. I decided to ride at my own rhythm until about five kilometres from the top and then give it everything. At first Loro and Roux were with me. Close to the summit I left the two of them as I went after Delgado. My Tour depended on getting close to him. This was not the day I won the Tour – but it was the day I saved it

➤ At the line I was totally exhausted. I stretched out a hand for support but there was nothing there. I waited for somebody to take hold of my bike but nobody would. Eventually Patrick undid my toe strap and I just fell. I had no force in my arms, nothing in my legs. I remember Patrick telling me that my legs were crossed and that I should straighten them before I was trampled on. I tried but my legs would not respond. I was aware that the doctor was over me and putting a mask over my face. I was not sure it was oxygen. But soon I was feeling better and my only worry was whether I would be 100 per cent fit the next day

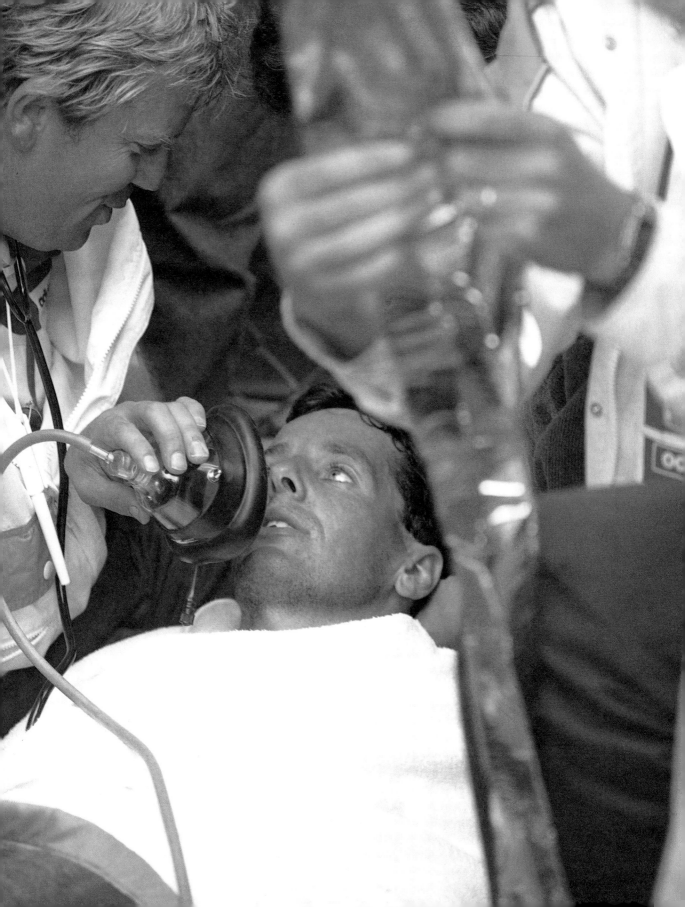

▲ After the collapse at La Plagne Eddy and I decided that on the next day's stage to Morzine he should try to be at my side all day. That is precisely what he did. At this point on the Joux Plane (the final climb of the stage) there was, from left, Delgado, Eddy, Lejarreta, Parra and I. Eddy was very strong and I reckoned that, for once, I was stronger on the climbs than Delgado

➤ Having taken the jersey from Delgado in Dijon I had only to protect it on the final stage to Paris. Normally nobody tries anything on this stage and, thankfully, that was the case this year. My team mates rode at the front and we had no problems

➤ On the descent into Morzine I got away from Delgado. With the yellow jersey on his back he chased desperately all the way to the finish line in Morzine but was still 18 seconds behind me where it counted. The 18 seconds were important in that they reduced my deficit from 39 seconds to 21. Psychologically it was a very important gain for me. It was likely that I would beat Delgado by more than 21 seconds in the 38-kilometre Dijon time trial on the second-last day

Being in the yellow jersey on the final day of the Tour meant a series of different feelings during the day. In the morning I felt reasonably sure I would win, but not absolutely. I remember going to the front of the peloton on the neutralized part of the stage (that is, the few kilometres we ride before the actual start) and posing for photographs with Jean Paul van Poppel who had the green jersey. Everybody presumed it was all over but not me. I felt much better when it came round to meeting the Irish Prime Minister Charlie Haughey on the Champs Elysées and then taking a drink in the medical control caravan

▲ Lydia does so much to make things work for me. She knows that it is not possible for her to be on the races but it is good for me to see her on the big races occasionally and it is nice when she can share in the limelight

► The Champs Elysées and the final podium. Over the final week the battle with Delgado had been hard but without any ill-feeling. At the end there was a sincere handshake. Well done! Well done! He had no complaints and neither had I!

▲ Talking to the journalists after a big success presents me with no difficulties. When I was going through the bad times I always tried to maintain a courteous relationship with them and when things started to go better and I began to win some important races the journalists did not forget that I had always been helpful to them. They were very kind to me after I won the Tour

Coming home to Dublin and showing the yellow
jersey to a quarter of a million fans gave me one
of the greatest thrills of my life. Lydia had a good
time as well

ITALY, FRANCE AND NOW—

THE WORLD!

RIDING
FOR
KELLY

As soon as the Tour de France was over there were some people who wondered whether I could win the World Championship as well. Not that many, but there were some. It was said that only one rider in the history of the sport, Merckx in 1974, had won the tours of Italy and France and the world title in the same year.

Could I join Merckx as the second man to win all three? I did not think so. In fact I did not know that Merckx had been the only one to win all three in the same season. All I knew was that I was very tired after two long tours and did not have the morale to begin serious preparation for the Worlds.

One of the television stations asked Merckx about the Villach circuit in Austria and he said it was one that would suit the sprinters, Vanderaerden and Van Poppel. Merckx can sometimes be wrong but his view of the circuit was enough to convince me that I would not be suited to the Villach course.

I did not find it easy to prepare for the world race. I could not find the motivation to go for the five- and six-hour training rides which are necessary to get oneself ready for it. I was tired and did not consider that I had a real chance of becoming world champion.

Five weeks passed between the end of the Tour and the world championship. In the week after the Tour ended I rode a couple of criteriums in Holland and then one in Belgium. The Belgian race went over the Mur de Grammont and I came out of it with a strained calf muscle.

It was not a serious injury but I interpreted it as a message from my body to slow down, to take a break. So I rested for five days. I then went with Lydia and the kids to Ile d'Oleron near Bordeaux, and spent another few days there.

While there I got back on the bike and did a couple of hard spins, about four or five hours each. It was very hot and I was exhausted by the time I finished. I returned to Paris and spent another week recovering from the Tour and trying to think of the Worlds.

I still did not have the morale for long training spins and, although I trained each day, I could only stay out for an hour and a half to two hours. Three weeks had passed since the Tour ended and I had lost the condition I had in the Tour. I was not looking forward to a seven-hour ride in the world road race.

Exactly two weeks before the Worlds, I returned to serious competition by riding the Three Valleys race in Italy. I found it very hard but I finished it. I rode as you would expect a semi-fit cyclist to ride and at the end of the race had absolutely nothing left.

After Italy I went to Ireland for three criteriums: Dublin, Wexford and Cork. Although they were just one-hour races, the week in Ireland was well spent. I linked up with Kelly, Earley and Kimmage and we trained together as well as riding the criteriums.

The four of us got on really well and as we would be wearing green jerseys together in the world championship it was good for us to be together. We had fun. I could feel myself coming round and after leaving Ireland I went to Italy for my final preparation.

I began to feel that I could do a ride for Sean, who was very keen to produce a good performance in Villach. As the days passed and the world race got nearer, I felt myself getting better all the time. I was pretty sure that I would be able to help Sean.

For almost half the race the rain pelted down on us, making conditions very dangerous and discouraging people from breaking away. The rain helped Sean and me, not because we like riding in the rain but because it lowered the spirits of so many others. We knew that most of the French and Italian stars would not like the conditions

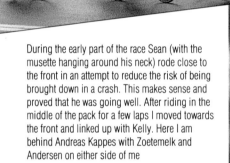

During the early part of the race Sean (with the musette hanging around his neck) rode close to the front in an attempt to reduce the risk of being brought down in a crash. This makes sense and proved that he was going well. After riding in the middle of the pack for a few laps I moved towards the front and linked up with Kelly. Here I am behind Andreas Kappes with Zoetemelk and Andersen on either side of me

What was achieved in Austria was based on the work of the team. Both Martin (right) and Paul rode very well and very courageously. We had spent a week together in Ireland before the race and we got on fine. It was very encouraging for Kelly and me that Martin and Paul were so much behind us

The Italian team was strong, as we expected it to
be. They controlled the race for long periods. My
Carrera team mate Bruno Leali is one of the best
team riders in the business and can ride at the
front for long stretches. Then there is Moser, still
a very strong man. There was talk that I would
ride the Barrachi Trophy with Moser but that
would mean special training for me and I was not
interested

◄ Argentin leads the pack. I had raced against him four days previously in Italy and he was flying. On the last hill of that race he just took off and zoomed away from all of us. He impressed me. Before starting out in the World Championship race I regarded him as the big favourite

▲ One of the first breakaways of any importance was made by the Dane Johnny Weltz and the Norwegian Janus Kuum. The difficulty with going early in the World Championship is that the chasing pack is still full of strength. Weltz and Kuum gave it everything but they never had a chance

119

▲ When Argentin and Van Vliet escaped in a four-rider group four laps from the end, different people took part in the pursuit. Laurent Fignon was one of the strongest and played a part in the recapture. Fignon is quiet but I like him. He has a presence in the peloton

➤ Over the second half of the race I began to feel better and better. I could see that Sean was going well and that everything was going to plan. What we had to ensure was that he arrived at the finish with the leaders and I did not mind riding hard to ensure this happened

A FINE MESS!

With about three kilometres to go, everything was perfect. Sean and I were in the leading group and it seemed sure that the gold medal would fall to one of our group. It looked really good for Sean, with his sprint, he was the big favourite.

From the start the race had gone our way. Although there were only five on the Irish team we had set out to help Sean get to the finish in a winning position. Alan McCormack, who had travelled from America, could not go well in the

rain but the rest of us (Kelly, Earley and Kimmage) were able to survive it pretty well.

Although the circuit was not very severe it was difficult enough and it was very hard for people to escape from the peloton. The Italian team was strong, as were the Dutch, and they each had one of the strongest riders in the race in Moreno Argentin and Van Vliet.

Argentin was the reigning champion and had the complete backing of the Italian squad, while the

Dutch were behind Van Vliet. When, four laps from the end, Argentin and Van Vliet attacked with Fernandez and Nevers everybody was worried that they would never be recaptured.

Fignon and Mottet rode hard in pursuit, I did a good turn at the front and so did Martin (Earley).

Once we brought them back I then tried to keep things together for Sean. With one lap to go I was worried that Sean might be beaten by Vanderaerden or Bontempi, two of the fastest sprinters, who were still in the bunch of about 70.

So I rode very strongly on the climb. I was surprised to find that the bunch split and only twelve were able to follow. Sean and I then had to control the other eleven, who were not enthusiastic about arriving to the finish in the company of Sean.

Everything went well until about two kilometres from the finish. Then there was a split, five of us at the front, the other eight about 300 metres behind, I kept looking back, waiting for Sean to rejoin us. With one kilometre to go I looked back and still there was no sign of Sean. I thought to myself, 'This is another fine mess you've got me into, Kelly.'

When the final split came two kilometres from the finish and Sean was caught in the wrong part of the lead group, I had visions of finishing fourth or fifth in the sprint of five. More than anything else I did not want that. I had to attack. What a feeling it was to look back and see that I had made a clean escape!

TAKING THE BULL BY THE HORNS!

When I was sure that Kelly was not going to rejoin us at the front I began to think about my own situation. In a sprint of five I was not going to do any better than third. Van Vliet and Goiz are better than me in the sprint.

The only way I could win was by breaking away from the group before the sprint began. I had to take the bull by the horns. I was in fourth place, behind Sorensen, Van Vliet and Golz. Winterberg was the only one behind me.

There was a narrow gap between the line of three riders and the barrier on the left side of the road. I went through it and gave it everything. After keeping the effort going for about 200 metres I had a look behind to see who was on my wheel. I was surprised to find there was nobody there.

I looked again, still nobody. I checked again, first left and then right. I had got clean away. I was going to win the world title. I surged again. Towards the end the rise to the line got steeper and I could not turn the big gear I was in. But I had gained enough of an advantage to hold on.

Then there was euphoria. The presentation of the gold medal and rainbow jersey, the interviews and the get together that evening with the three lads and the Irish supporters who had come to cheer us on. It was a good night.

The victory was so sweet because it was so unexpected. I had not even contemplated the prospect of winning until I made the final attack 450 metres from the line. Those are the hands of Herman Nys, the man with whom Sean lived for about six years in Brussels. Herman has always been a great friend to Sean and me

They say the camera never lies. Then why I am looking so serious as I wait to get the world championship gold medal and rainbow jersey. I will wear the rainbow jersey all through 1988 and will be instantly recognized. There is a responsibility that comes with the rainbow jersey

The expression is now what you would expect it to be. I felt a little tired after the race but not especially so. There was a good feel to the rainbow jersey. Ah, World Champion!

Meeting the journalists afterwards was good fun and far better organized than the Tour de France or Tour of Italy. Why can it not be like this on the tours? The interview was conducted in three languages: French, Italian and English. I acted as both interviewee and translator! I think it is important to have a good relationship with the journalists, it is a part of being a professional

After the presentation there was an interview for Irish television. Explaining how I had not expected to win, how pleased I was to have won and, generally, savouring the occasion